THE

THE COWHERDING PARABLE AND THE UNKILLABLE HUMAN

Frederick Franck

Royal Fireworks Press
Unionville, New York

Toronto, Ontario

In gratitude to my friends

Dean and Marcia Nims,
Helen Boyle,
Mary Boyle,
to John Lewis Stage, who photographed this work,
to Dea Archbold and JoAnn Mannino
of Sundog Glass Studio,
to Albin Elskus, eminent stained glass artist
who initiated me in the craft,
to Gerard O'Brien, oldest friend of Pacem in Terris,
to Thomas Kemnitz who printed this book,
to Arthur Meyer who built "The Other Shore,"
but first and foremost
to Claske Berndes Franck
without her neither this
nor anything else
is thinkable

frederick franck

Copyright ©1996, Frederick Franck.
All Rights Reserved.

Royal Fireworks Press
First Avenue
Unionville, NY 10988
(914) 726-4444
FAX: (914) 726-3824

Royal Fireworks Press
78 Biddeford Avenue
Downsview, Ontario
M3H 1K4 Canada
FAX: (416) 633-3010

ISBN: 0-88092-222-2

Printed in the United States of America on acid-free, recycled paper using vegetable-based inks by the Royal Fireworks Press of Unionville, New York.

THE TAO OF THE CROSS, THE OXHERDING PARABLE, AND THE UNKILLABLE HUMAN

For me it started more than eighty years ago. In those years, the news has become so repetitious as to be hackneyed: ... "tanks crossing borders" ... "oil wells bombed"... "heavy civilian casualties"... "aircraft carriers ordered to"...

I was born on the Dutch-Belgian border, and was five years old, when on August 4, 1914, I was awakened by the roar of field guns. Kaiser Wilhelm's armies had invaded Belgium less than a mile from our doorstep. The next town, across the border, stood in flames. At once a continuous stream of wounded and dying soldiers on blood-stained stretchers, pushcarts, horse-drawn wagons, endless throngs of people fleeing their burning villages poured across the frontier into Holland which managed to stay neutral in World War I.

From my fifth to my ninth year, peering from our neutral grandstand into hell, I developed the violent allergy against wars, killings, violence I would never overcome, and with it started a life-long questioning about what it might mean to be human.

My father being agnostic, we lived on a little agnostic island in the ocean of a Catholic culture that straddled the border. "If I live a decent life," he said, "should there be a hereafter—God or no God—I don't have to fear what can happen to me." I did not inherit his agnostic temperament. As by osmosis I absorbed the symbols of the surrounding Catholic culture. They served as the core around which first intimations of Meaning, of the Transcendent could crystallize.

Crucifixes, Madonna shrines stood on every crossroad, beacons in the Catholic ocean. Nuns were always herding little children through the neat park surrounding a famous "Calvary": a row of fourteen grottos, fieldstone and cement. In each one stood a gaudy plaster sculpture depicting a Station of the Cross, the suffering Christ surrounded by sobbing, hand-wringing women who, in one of the last grottos, sustained a swooning Virgin Mary, her skyblue cloak undone, her heart pierced by swords.

Closer to home, on the Cathedral wall the naked man was hanging, dying forever, pale hands and feet pierced by nails, blood trickling from crown of thorns and chest. I passed him twice a day on my way to and from school. Wasn't there some mysterious link between him and those soldiers dying on pushcarts, the wretched fugitives carrying their children on their backs, were they not as heartrendingly vulnerable, as human... as human as I? At the end of the Calvary he was entombed under a huge boulder, and that was the end of him. Or was it? For on Easter Sunday, with all church bells clanging, a solemn procession with velvet banners and brass bands, a hundred angels flapping tulle wings, priests in white albs swinging incense burners, shuffling notables in top hats, wound its way through our streets to celebrate his Resurrection. He was risen! He was obviously unkillable, the Unkillable Human!

I wonder how old I was when I invented a symbol of my own. It was derived from the story that the fish was the oldest symbol of Christ "ever since the catacombs" as was always added. A bit later, somehow, I must have picked up the term "Mystical Body of Christ". I had no idea what that might mean, but it had a musical ring, like an organ chord. Both images fused together into an immense Fish, turquoise and silver. From each one of its million scales a human face was looking out, white, black, yellow, live and dead faces. If you looked very intensely there were even squirrels, mice, insects peering at you. I saw the great Fish swimming, sailing, through the heavens, through the interstellar spaces. It must have been much later that I called it the Cosmic Fish. This Cosmic Fish never lost its meaning, on the contrary. When a life-time later I read about the "total interdependence of all phenomena in the Universe" as it is formulated in the 7th Century Chinese Hua Yen School of Buddhism—known as Kegon in Japan—I recognized in my Cosmic Fish a symbol that was as Buddhist as it was Catholic. I have drawn it, painted it, sculpted it in stone, in wood, and a year or so ago I forged it, quite large, in steel. It must be the Cosmic Fish that prevented me from "joining" anything, from allegiance to any in-group, any political party, church, sect or clique. I was to remain a loner in allegiance to the Fish, my all encompassing Fish.

I was to outlive almost the full length of this 20th century that only began in earnest on that 4th of August 1914 when, on the pretext of the murder of an Austrian archduke in Sarajevo, the First Great Bloodletting exploded. It is sheer miracle to be still here, as the century is drawing to its close with Sarajevo once more in the headlines. Ever since that fateful August day, it had been a continuum of massacres, of subhuman savagery, of the manic desecration of life. It leapt from the insane battles of the Marne, Ypres and Verdun—400.000 corpses in one day—via Guernica to the massacres of Rotterdam, Dresden, My Lai, Mogadishu, Kigali. It tolerated the unfathomable evil of Auschwitz, Birkenau and—having learned nothing—fifty years later, that of Mostar, Srebrenica. It staged at Hiroshima-Nagasaki a preview of our species' auto-crucifixion, with no resurrection to follow. The Way of the Cross was never further away in this long life than the next newscast.

I am not sure now at which one of these trigger points of horror, some years ago, the stark images of the Way of the Cross, etched on the inner eye in childhood, sprang to life. It made me grab a brush and give it form, black ink on large sheets of white paper. Stripped to its bare essentials, it was a series of fifteen "close-ups" of the Human face, the "Face of faces" as the 14th Century mystic Nicholas of Cusa called it. The face that is "Human beyond description."

It is miracle enough to have survived this century-long pandemic of rabies afflicting the human mind. Still, even more wondrous is it to have not only seen, but to have experienced first hand, amidst the non-stop bedlam, those innumerable acts of humanness, of compassion, mercy and tenderness that kept, despite all, my faith in what is human in humans more alive than ever. I was moreover privileged to meet the three old men who embodied this humanness most compellingly: Albert Schweitzer, the Protestant doctor who lived his credo of "Reverence for Life" to the full, Pope John XXIII, the Catholic pope whose courage, freedom, tenderness and humor proved to be as unkillable as his Master, and Daisetz T. Suzuki, the Buddhist sage who almost single-handedly initiated the West into Zen, into Buddhism's "Wisdom that is Compassion, the Compassion that is Wisdom."

They were the living embodiments of that humanness that speaks out of works of high art, Rembrandt's Emmaus, his self-portraits, out of all that Bach ever wrote, Beethoven's last Quartets, Rilke's Sonnets.

But I also was to meet it constantly in ordinary people wherever I went, whether in this country, Europe or Japan, and these days more frequently than ever before. Everywhere people seem more likely to switch from conventional small talk to such matters as the roots of evil and violence, the fate of the earth. They dare speak more openly of the soul, of Meaning, of the Spirit, than even ten years ago.

Could it possibly herald a quantum leap in our collective consciousness, a turnabout from a de-humanized, materialistic, mechanistic mentality, to that which may still save us. For what can still save us is the rediscovery of the human in us as having absolute priority, in comparison with which all our problems are secondary, be they economic, political or technological: Signs of the Unkillable Human?

Here I must stop thinking aloud and take you on a detour, for the story of both my Way of the Cross windows and those of the Parable of the Oxherd is inseparable from the story of Pacem in Terris. It starts with a winter hike through the hills around Warwick, N.Y. some thirtyfive years ago. We crossed a little bridge and spotted the wreck of a house. Its mortal remains were leaning awry on the banks of a river. It was love at first sight: not only was the Wawayanda the spitting image of the river that ran behind my great-grandfather's house, the hilly landscape mirrored that of the borderland of my childhood.

The house had a taciturn dignity of its own. We could not get close to it through the deep snow, but found an estate agent who told us that it dated back to around 1840 and had once been a tavern, "McCann's Saloon." We bought it for a song, sight unseen, pulled it straight, restored it, emigrated from Greenwich Village and moved in. The first winter we spent in McCann's Saloon we were astonished to see that the trash heap across the river, camouflaged in summer by a jungle of poison ivy and sumac, was enclosed in massive walls of fieldstone. It was the ruin of a late 18th Century grist mill, as we found out when we became the proud owners of an authentic early-American garbage dump.

A dump is all it would still be, were it not for Pope John XXIII. But this may require some elucidation.

On October 12, 1962, soon after our return from Lambarene, after three years on the Equator where we had served on the medical staff of Albert Schweitzer's legendary jungle hospital, I was walking up Fifth Avenue to an appointment while leafing through the New York Times, but stopped suddenly in my tracks, when my eye fell on Pope John's epoch-making, profoundly moving opening address to the Second Vatican Council he had convoked. I was so thunderstruck by this *vox humana* sounding out, of all places, the Vatican, that I called off my appointment, ran home and told Claske: "We are off to Rome! Read this! This is going to be a watershed! I have to draw that man and his Council! He is much more than a pope, he is a prophet, he must be a *mensch!*"

It was easier said than done. The confab of some two thousand bishops and cardinals in St. Peter's was a tightly closed shop. How I, neither cardinal, nor bishop, nor even card-carrying Catholic, could gate-crash it and draw the drama, its author and its main actors during the Council's four autumn sessions from 1962-1964, I can not go into here. But neither can I explain it, for it was sheer miracle, as I came to see everything that ever "worked" in my life as "sheer miracle," for whatever I calculated and planned however cleverly, backfired.

Was not outliving Hitler and Stalin sheer miracle? Or finding among a billion women Claske, without whom McCann's Saloon, Pacem in Terris, drawing

Schweitzer and his hospital, Pope John and his Vatican II, plus everything else that has been good in life would be unthinkable?

One may babble about karma, coincidence, hold forth on destiny and even synchronicity, but these are no more than synonyms for what is as awesomely miraculous as life itself. One of these miracles, perhaps the most puzzling, happened on June 3, 1963 when all day we listened to the radio, following Pope John's long agony. until in mid afternoon the news came that he had died. Only then did we open the mail and in it was a letter from Rome announcing that it had "pleased the Holy Father to confer" on me, in appreciation of my drawings of the First Session of the Council—they had been widely reproduced—the Medal of His Pontificate. It was too much!

We drove to Kennedy that night and flew to Rome. I had to draw this genius of the heart, this Bodhisattva Pope, this manifestation of the Spirit in our time, once more on his bier. I can not think of anyone I loved more than Angelo Roncalli, John XXIII.

When after the funeral we flew home and I saw our mill ruin across the Wawayanda again, I knew what I had to do. It designed itself in a flash. I saw the modern roof that was to crown these old stone walls that recalled a medieval priory in Dordogne. The roof, seen from every angle, would symbolize the winging of the Dove... I was going to make my early-American garbage dump into a trans-religious sacred place that might resonate with the sacred space in the human heart. It would be a work of art, but one outside of the art game, a spiritual statement outside of all religious games, independent from any religious, cultic, political, ideological institution or organization.

We decided not to ask anyone's advice or money, we would manage. Claske took a job that paid for materials and the wages of Bert Willemse who had also restored McCann's Saloon. He was to be my only helper. Even before we started to dig out the twelve hundred wheelbarrows of debris—machinery would have destroyed the ancient walls—I had called it "Pacem in Terris" after Pope John's noble encyclical written on the threshold of death. As the design had come spontaneously, so did the sculptures in wood and steel, the mosaics as well as the stained glass windows I made —and had to remake for the first ones, one night, were destroyed by vandals.

Pacem in Terris would be dedicated to the spirit of the three old men, first of all to the Catholic Pope who had been a prophet of human solidarity, but no less to Albert Schweitzer, the Protestant doctor and to the Buddhist sage Suzuki. We repaired the walls, reconstructed the almost romanesque doorway on the level of the Wawayanda. Bert, all by himself, and without a crane, built the roof, which peaks 45 feet above water level, and the 57 foot truss that supports it.

We opened Pacem in 1966 to whomsoever it might have something to say, and through the years there have been thousands. It never was "finished." There is always something to add, be it a sculpture, a bench hewn out of a blown-over oak, an organic flower-and-vegetable garden to show what Mother Earth will do, given half a chance. There was of course never an admission charge to this oasis of quiet, of the beauty of old stones, of trees and water. Chamber music concerts came about when musicians were fascinated by Pacem's atmosphere and its unplanned, yet extraordinary acoustics.

Pacem has no "members," it is simply open to all from May till October. We never applied for foundation grants except for a little seed money in the very beginning, and yet Pacem has never been in the red. It has been self-sustaining—in itself no small miracle—by subscriptions to The Shoestring, its newsletter, plus the unsollicited donations that come from people of every religious affiliation or none. Its overheads are minimal for we do all the work ourselves with the help of a handful of volunteers. My son, Lukas, volunteer par excellence notwithstanding his intense work with the blind—he has been on the teaching staff of the Seeing Eye Foundation for the past fifteen years. He also led the traditional New Year's celebration based on a Tibetan ceremony for a number of years and directed performances of "The Death and Life of EveryOne," my contemporary variation on the theme of the medieval Play of Everyman.

In 1972 Pacem obtained not-for-profit status. Nevertheless its profits have been astronomical in letters and words of appreciation and fellow feeling, in human contacts and relationships. Pacem has no other ambition than to witness to the human in human beings, and to an attitude to Life as being sacred: a "religious" orientation to sheer Existence as the great Mystery. Bert died some twenty years ago. Soon after, again somewhat miraculously, Arthur Meyer, an extraordinarily versatile and creative craftsman came to Pacem. Without Art's skills, maintenance would have been impossible, my steel icons could not have happened, nor "The Other Shore," the little sanctuary that houses the stained glass windows, and which he built all by himself.

Here, at last, comes the link between Pacem in Terris and the stained glass windows that are the subject of this book. They started with a phone call last Spring from Des Moines, Iowa: "Mr. Nims would like to speak to you. Hold on, please." I never met Dean Nims face to face, but for years he has been one of the most generous supporters of Pacem in Terris. "I have been thinking" he started, "about your black and white 'Way of the Cross' and those 'Oxherding Pictures.' When I saw them in the Cathedral of St. John the Divine they touched me very much and so I wondered: Have you ever thought of translating them into stained glass?"

I was stunned for a moment. This black and white Way of the Cross I had brushed ink on paper, in a kind of trance, in shock almost at one of those outbursts of sheer barbrism that are our regular media diet. I felt challenged. I had not worked in stained glass for years, although I love the medium. This was my chance. No subject could be more timely than doing this "translation" at the end of the Second Millenium Anno Domini, marked by the killing epidemics in Rwanda, Bosnia, Timor, Tibet, the Bronx...

"You give me a wonderful idea" I said. "May I think about it and find out where I could possibly realize it, for I don't have kilns and all that around. I'll call you back."

Since I painted the black and white Way of the Cross that now belongs to the Cathedral, I had come to see the two thousand year old story of the Passion as transcending the ancient Catholic devotion, saw it as being of trans-historical and even trans-cultural relevance. It was "catholic" indeed in the sense of being universal and never more so than for this century of suffering and death. It epitomized the Way, the Truth, the Life of the human inner process, addressed itself to Everyman regardless of gender and of credal demarcation lines. It bridged East and West. I called it The Tao of the Cross.

I took a long look at my Way of the Cross in St. John the Divine, of which the Dean of the Cathedral, James Parks Morton, wrote: *"...a precious moment in history that can present together the sacred images at the center of two distinct religious traditions... In this work we find the open heart of the Stations of the Cross and the quiet mind of the Oxherding Series represented as accessible states accessible to all men and women... a progress of the deepest kind."*

I would accept the challenge, for better or worse. Suddenly I remembered seeing a sign "Sundog Glass Studio" a few miles away in Sugar Loaf, N.Y. I might as well explore it.

I found two young women at work restoring a church window. They were clearly professionals. I showed them reproductions of the black and white images I intended to "translate" into stained glass. They were not only interested but enthusiastic about this "creative adventure." We figured out costs then and there.

I called Dean Nims, told him that I had found the place to work on this awesome project, and that for me it would be a labor of love, but that there were considerable expenses involved for materials, firing, leading, final fabrication and such. "I have the estimate and it is not low..." "Tell me," he said. There was a second of silence, then the voice from Des Moines said: "Shall I send you a check?" I couldn't believe my ears.

"Where do you plan to place the windows?" I still asked. "We can talk about that later, just go ahead. By the way: how about at Pacem in Terris?"

It took a full three months. Apart from the electric kilns I intended to use techniques that had hardly changed since the Middle Ages. I would avoid using any industrial colored glass, but start with colorless glass of various textures. I drew each one of the Stations on large sheets of paper, designed the patterns of segments to be leaded, transferred these to the glass, which was then cut according to the design. There was a total of well over four hundred such segments. Each of these was painted with vitreous "enamels" and stains, then fired at 1000 - 1200 degrees to bond colors to glass. Often segments were fired and refired three or four times until the exact tonality and texture I aimed at were obtained - mostly "grisailles", for I dislike the standard stained glass gaudiness of blood reds, sky blues and bright yellows.

These three months became a retreat, a continuous meditation, a self-confrontation. Painting those fourteen "close-ups" of the "Face of faces" was not a matter of reaching esthetic or decorative effects. It was a being in touch with the rock bottom of the human condition. There was in this dark sequence of fourteen scenes, only one single "humane"—that is human act, that of Veronica wiping his brow. All the rest was the infliction of indignities, pain and death.

Until in the fifteenth Station, the stony heart of darkness is shattered by the blinding light of the Resurrection, triumph of the Unkillable Human, the "Human beyond description and understanding." *

The riddles that had started to preoccupy me before even entering first grade: What is human? Who am I? seemed close to their solution, as I was working on these windows. The Way of the Cross with the Resurrection as its apotheosis appeared ever more to be a mirror of the human inner process and its fulfilment. Often the

Cosmic Fish came to mind and it amazed me how as a child I had dreamt up this symbol of absolute oneness in limitless differentiation, of the absolute interdependence of Being. In this three months-long meditation the confrontation with the face I was painting in these fifteen "close-ups" the face which the Christian mystic Nicholas of Cusa spoke of as the "Face of faces veiled as in a riddle in every human face," merged with what the 7th Century Chinese Hui Neng called the "Original Face," challenging his disciples: "Show me the Original Face you had before even your parents were born."

This "Original Face," this "Face of faces" must be that of the one who "was before Abraham was", that specifically Human face which must have appeared at that point of our evolution when the Naked Ape, the anthropoid, mutated into Anthropos, the human—the Adam of Genesis. This old Adam - Adam means "human being"—still tainted by the pre-human oddities of the Naked Ape, was to be the predecessor of the New Adam from whom the last of the pre-human oddities had dropped off, who was "Human beyond description and understanding." *

It would be absurd to consider the Ten Oxherding Pictures as "equal" or even "equivalent" to the Tao of the Cross. It has, however, proven to be a powerful catalyst to profound meditation on the human condition ever since 11th Century in China and later in Japan. It is ascribed to Zen master Kakuan, but two even earlier versions were found, one of five, the other of six images.

My Oxherding Parable consists of ten small windows of 10 x 10" in a free rendering of Kakuan's version, but without his long commentaries. Each one consists of three layers of glass of which the outer one carries the image and title painted on, and then burned into, the glass. The second and third layers are not painted but sandblasted, so that sandwiched together a silk-like texture is obtained.

The Parable starts with the oxherd erring in despair on a barren field: he has lost his ox, symbol of the True Self. He has violated his own innermost nature, and the parable traces its recovery which ends with the oxherd's full enlightenment as a Bodhisattva who, foregoing the beatitude of Nirvana, descends into the market place bestowing blessings, leading those still lost in darkness and delusion to their awakening to the really Real.

The Oxherding Parable in its Far Eastern idiom evokes the universal human journey from still pre-human confusion and delusion to the fullness of human consciousness, of the Unkillable Human.

That the mutation from Naked Ape to Human is more than a figment of the poetic imagination, I found confirmed by science—notwithstanding science's reputation of having failed to contribute anything of value to matters of Ultimate Meaning. It happened, a few years ago, when, at 37,000 feet above the Pacific, I was reading an essay about recent neuro-scientific research on the evolution of the human brain and how this brain of ours actually consists of a "trinity of brains."

The oldest, most centrally located component of this "triune brain", the essay said, is the 280 million years-old reptilian brain that still survives in us, fully alive and kicking: with all its automatisms of foraging, mating, fighting intact. This still so highly active reptilian brain is enveloped by successively the Old and the New Mammalian brain, of which the latter evolved into those twin hemispheres which constitute that remarkable computer in our skulls which enables us to think deductively, to calculate, to verbalize, but that is still quite deficient in feeling and intuition. Clever enough to invent steam engine and neutron bomb, it never wrote a Hamlet or composed a B-Minor Mass, which could never have come about without the next step, the most recent outcropping of our brain, known as "the prefrontal cortex". This prefrontal cortex is what "humanizes" us, allows us to be aware of our own life process, to be conscious of being alive and having to die. This, in turn, is at the origin of our capacity to become also aware of the life process in other creatures, to identify with their joy, their pain. This signals the first inklings of empathy. From empathy to compassion is but a step...

After billions of years of a dog-eat-dog universe something new had appeared under the sun: the anthropoid, the Naked Ape—it bears repeating—had mutated into Anthropos, the Human. The humanizing capabilities of the pre-frontal cortex are as genetically encoded in us humans as are the ancient reptilian and mammalian automatisms, only more recently, and hence more precariously. I have described, what is here sketched out in a few words, in greater detail elsewhere.**

I believe it to be, and by far, the most momentous discovery of contemporary science: it tells us at last what it means to be human, who we humans really are, and where we fit into the cosmic Whole. It corroborates astonishingly, in the terms of modern science, the most profound intuitions of the pre-scientific mind, as laid down in the oldest spiritual and ethical traditions. It discloses our true identity beyond the false, narcissistic identities cherished by ego: to be human is to be capable of introspection, empathy, compassion and foresight. It illuminates at once what expressions like "the Sleeping Christ within" might really imply, as well as Buddhist references to the Original Face and the Buddha Nature, characterized as they are respectively by Christian love *(agape)* and wisdom *(sophia)* and Buddhist *(prajna)* (transcendent wisdom) and compassion *(karuna)*— unequal yet ultimately equivalent as these may be. Science thus supplies us with the criteria of what differentiates us from all other forms of life, and shows us our humanness as being genetically encoded in us, however subverted by all conditioning, by all programming by family, school, church and media. This constitutes the Magna Charta of the inviolable dignity of every one born human. Indeed this discovery of neuro-science is infinitely more important than all our technological wizardry taken together, for it justifies and restores those norms of human conduct without which no civilization can—or deserves to—survive....

It was the right moment for the intercom to announce that we were about to land at Kennedy. Blaring loudspeakers welcomed us, as we were carried up and down escalators, transported on the mile-long rubber conveyer belts from which I watched my "brothers and sisters" in their dazzling variety, gliding by in the opposite direction, and saw all of us equally addicted to the technological gadgetry, equally bamboozled by the superstition that technology has the solution for all that ails us, as if what ails us were not of an existential—or call it "spiritual"—nature, hence our addled priorities. What else could have first priority than the keen awareness that we are born human with the in-built assignment to become Human before we die? For unless we do, we have missed the boat, we have lived in vain. To go through life, behaving like crocodile or rat may routinely be rationalized as being "just human nature", but it is not, and has never been human nature, it is the rat-, the crocodile-nature in us running amuck, and which, outfitted with a high tech gone rabid, spells our species' demise with hydrogen bang or pollution whimper.

To be Human or not-to-be is, literally, the question.

*) "It is Easter Now," Jay G. Williams, Scriptoria Press, 1994

**) "To Be Human Against All Odds," Asian Humanities Press, 1991 - Royal Fireworks Press, 1996.

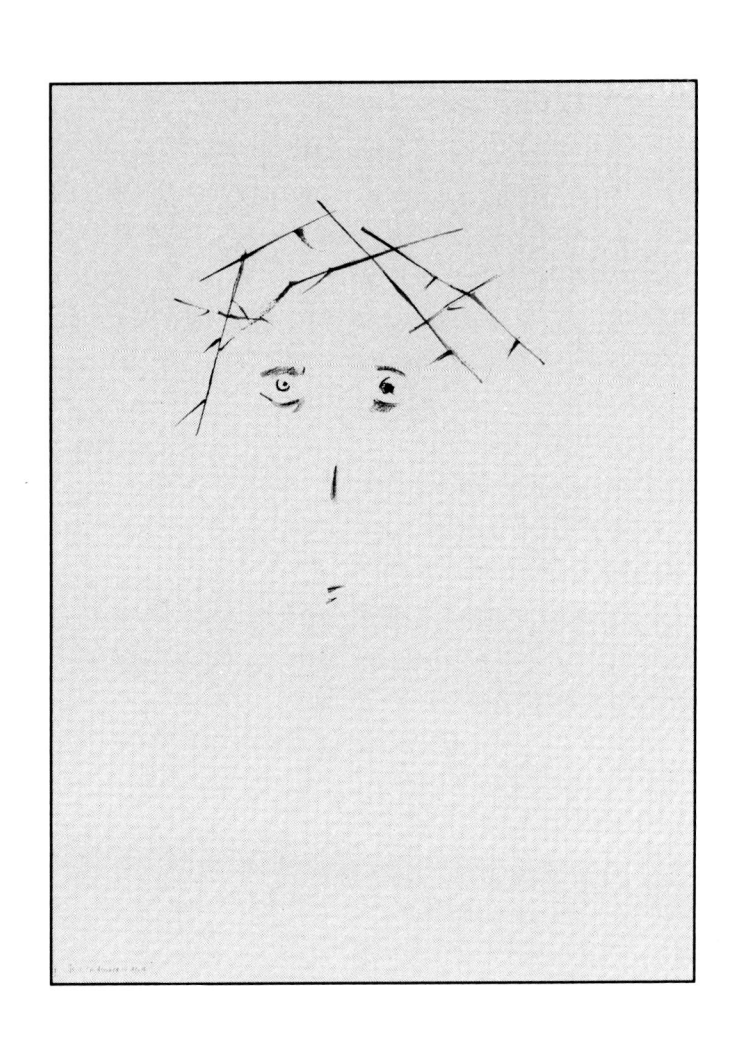

I Condemned To Death

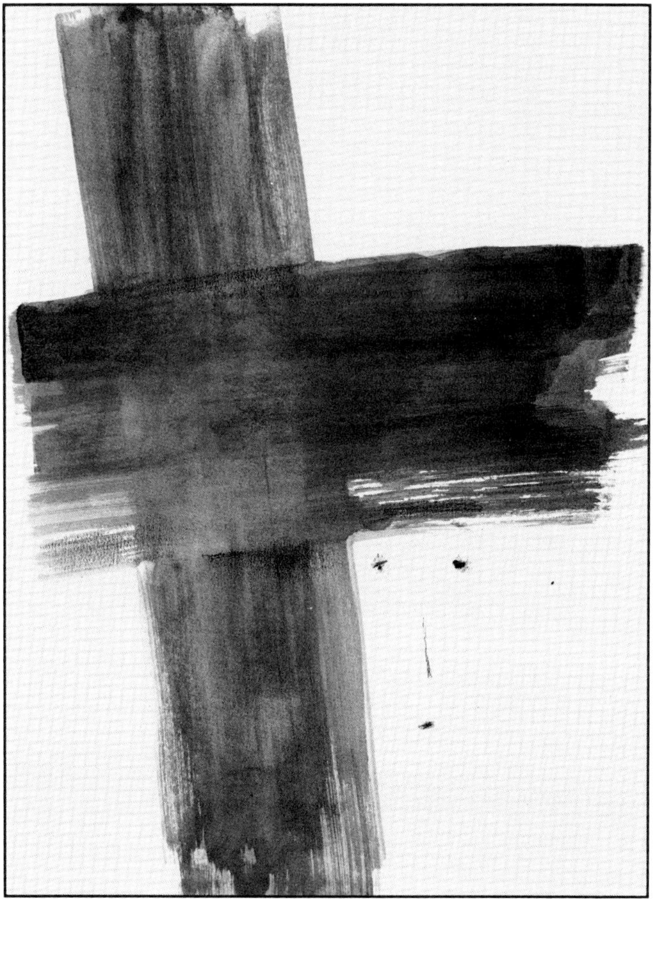

II Takes Up His Cross

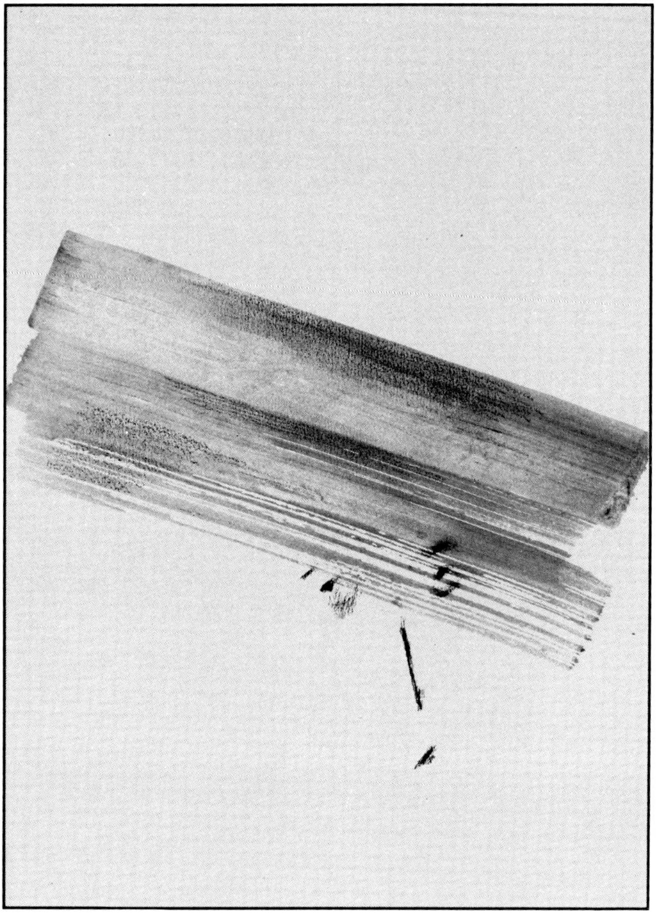

III He Falls The First Time

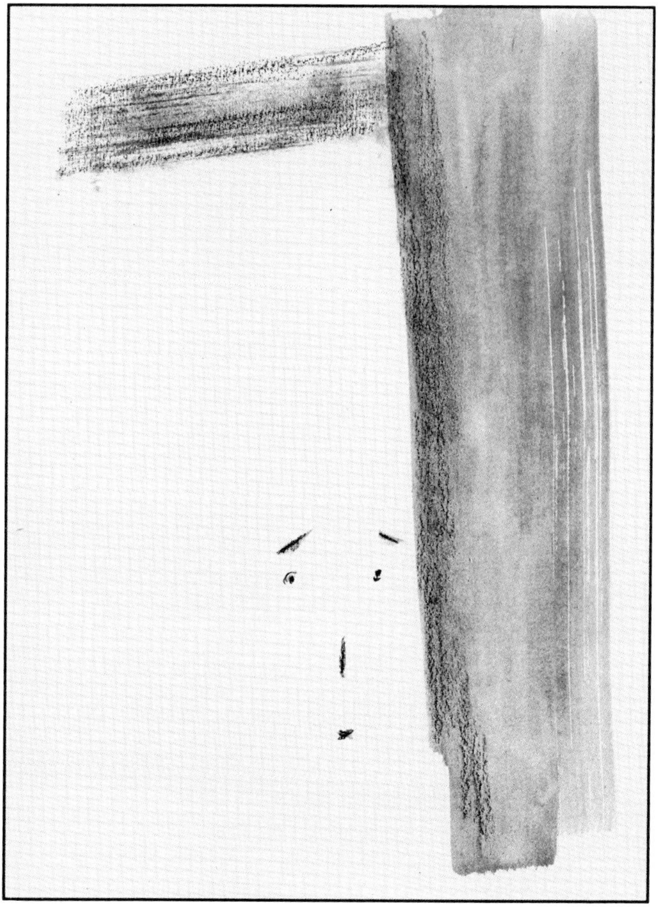

IV He Meets His Mother

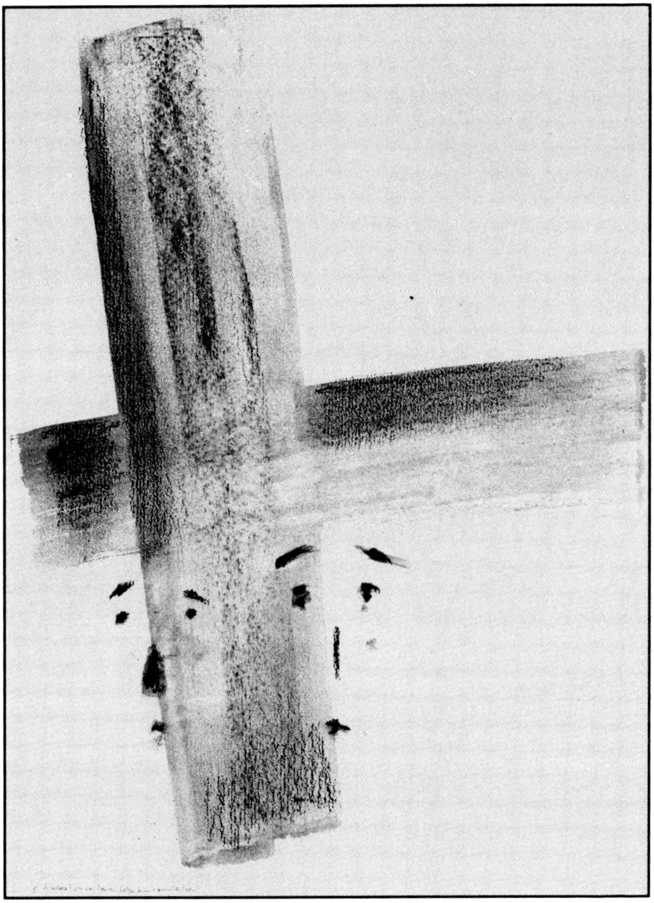

V Simon of Cyrene Helps Him Carry The Cross

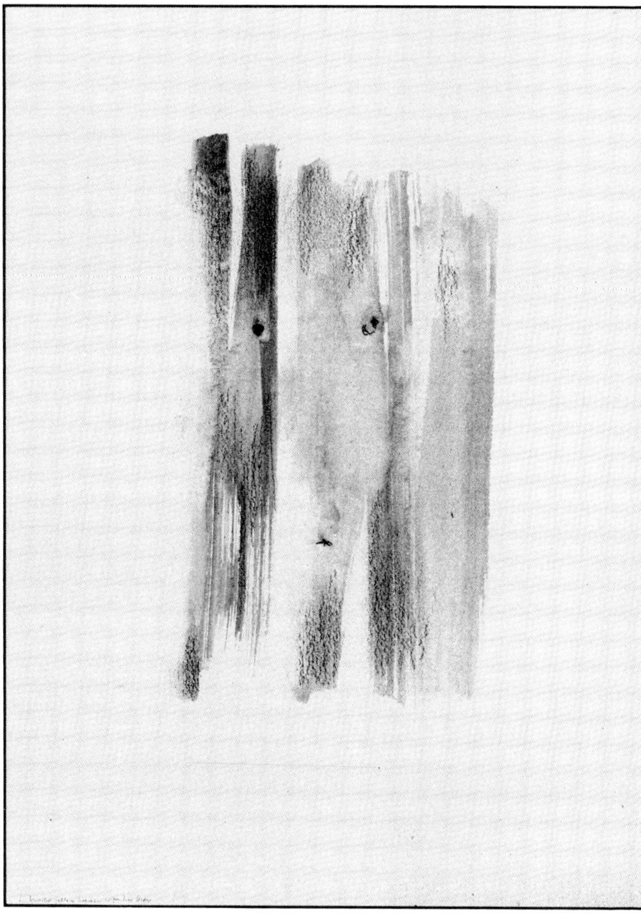

VI Veronica Wipes His Brow

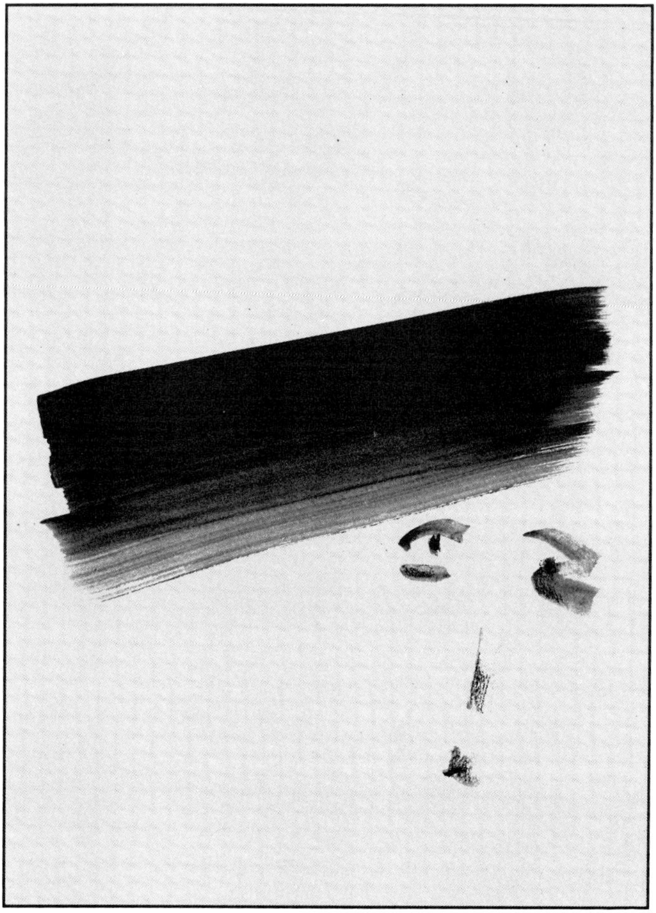

VII He Falls The Second Time

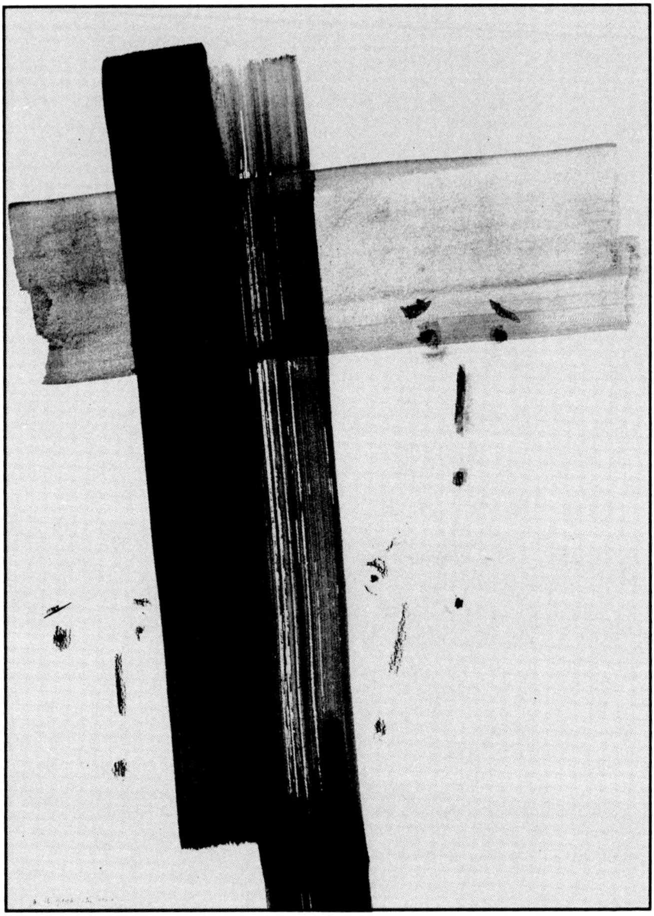

VIII   He Speaks To The Women

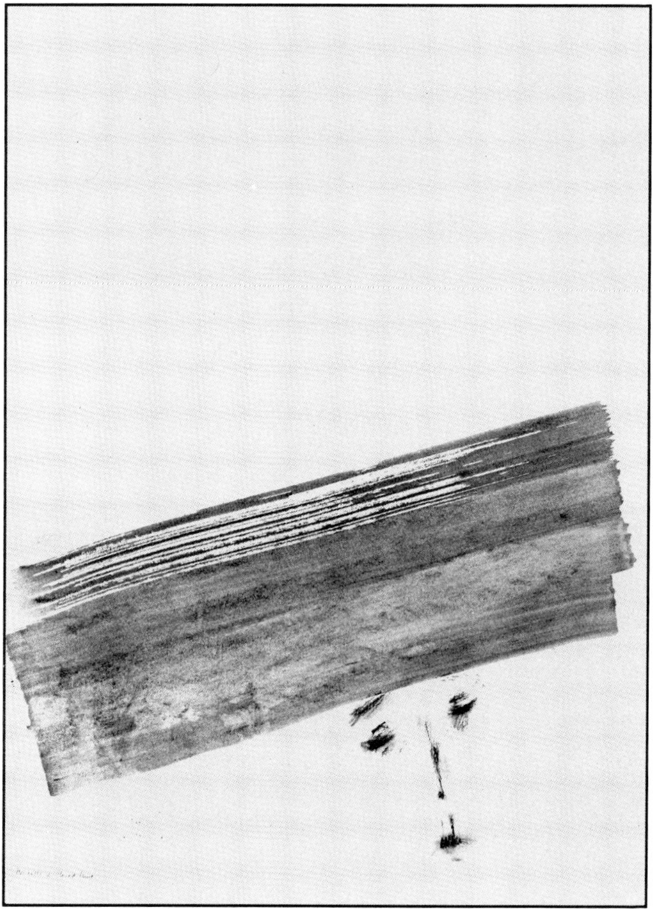

IX He Falls The Third Time

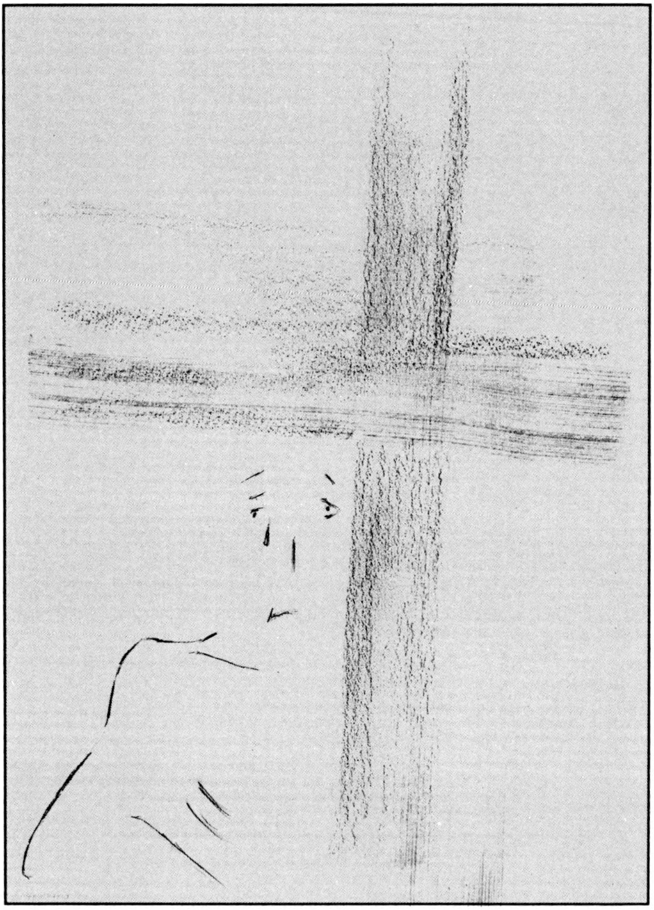

X He Is Stripped Naked

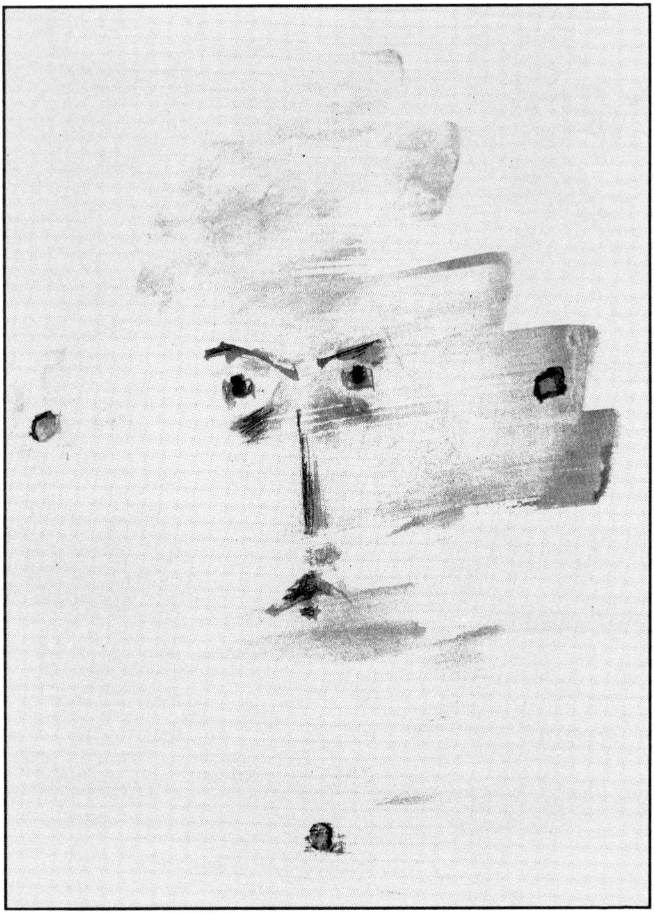

XI He Is Nailed To The Cross

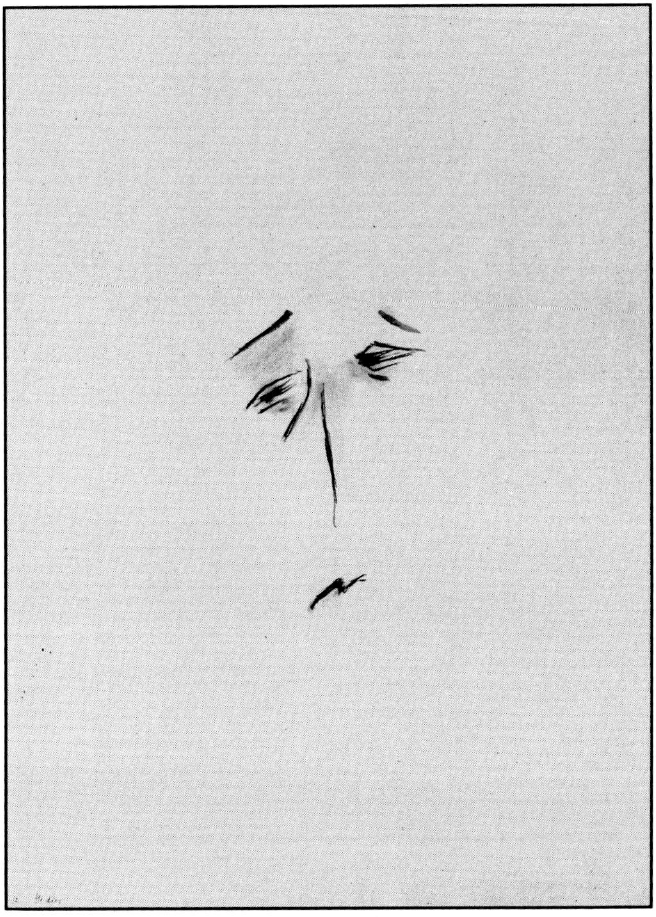

XII   He Dies

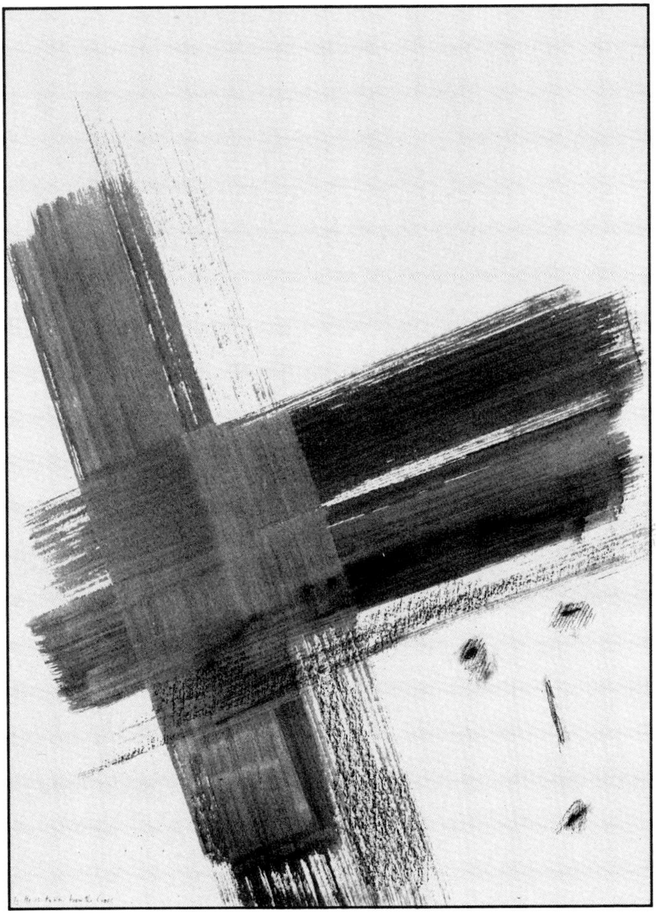

XIII He His Taken Off The Cross

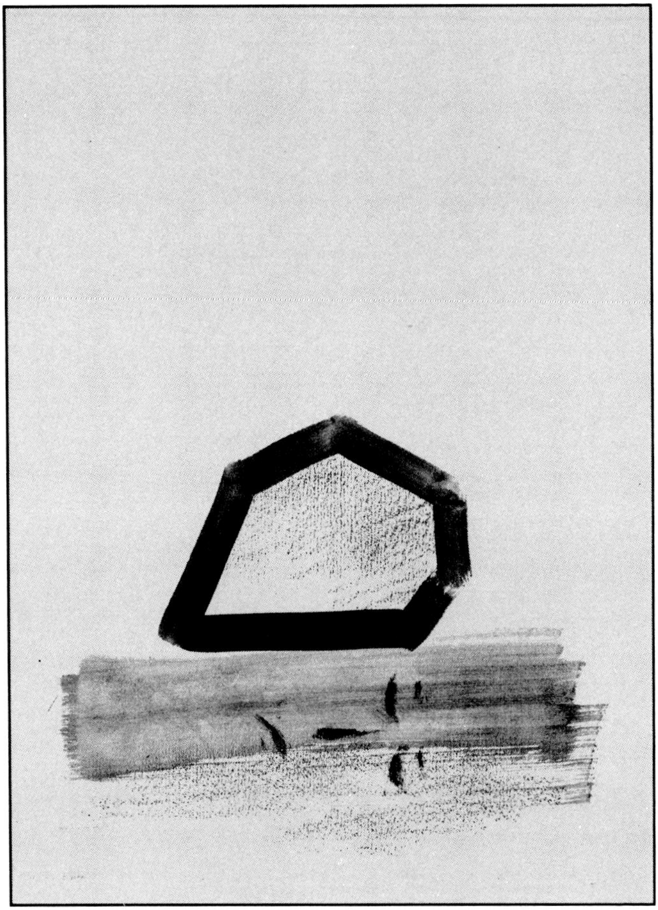

XIV He Is Buried

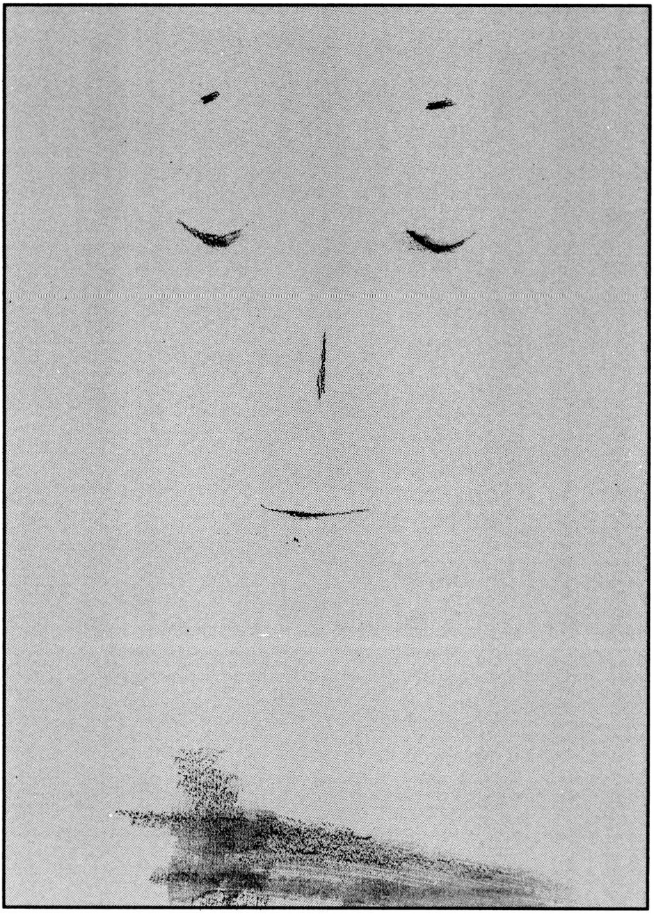

XV HE IS RISEN!

THE OXHERDING PARABLE

THE OX HERD HAS LOST HIS OX ...
(the true Self)

F.F.

HE ESPIES THE OX HOOFPRINTS

HE SEES THE OX, FAR AWAY...

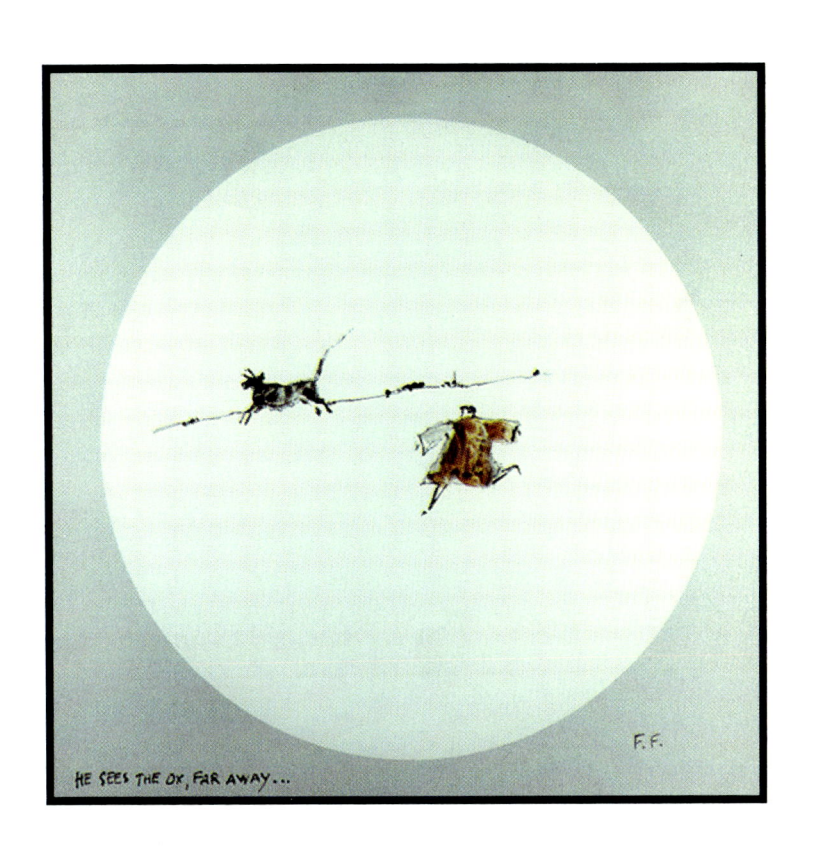

HE CATCHES THE OX

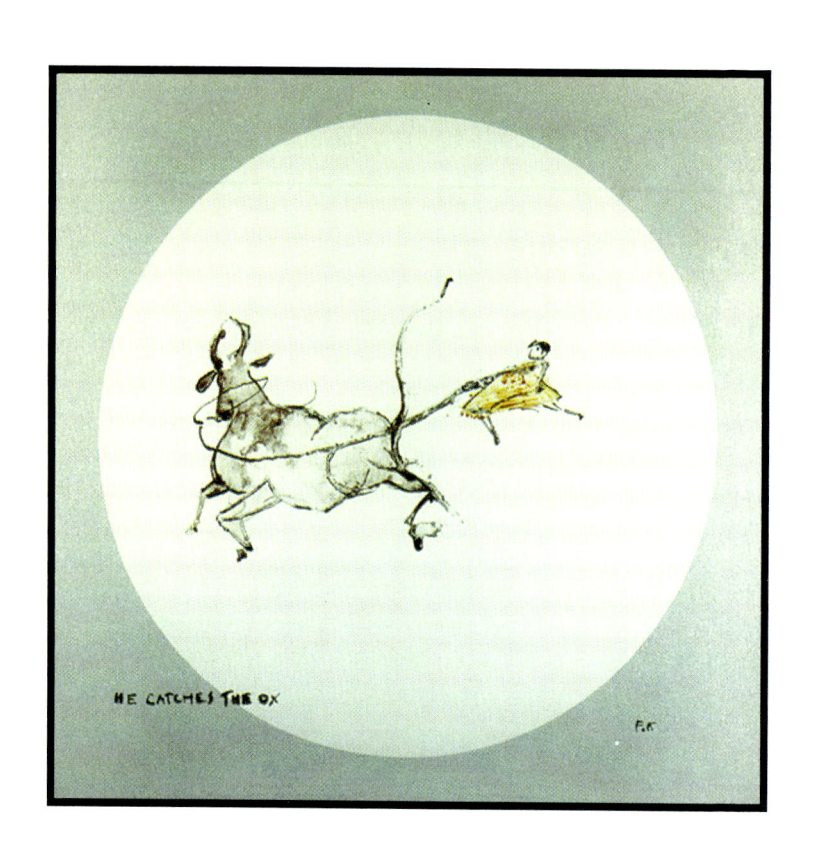

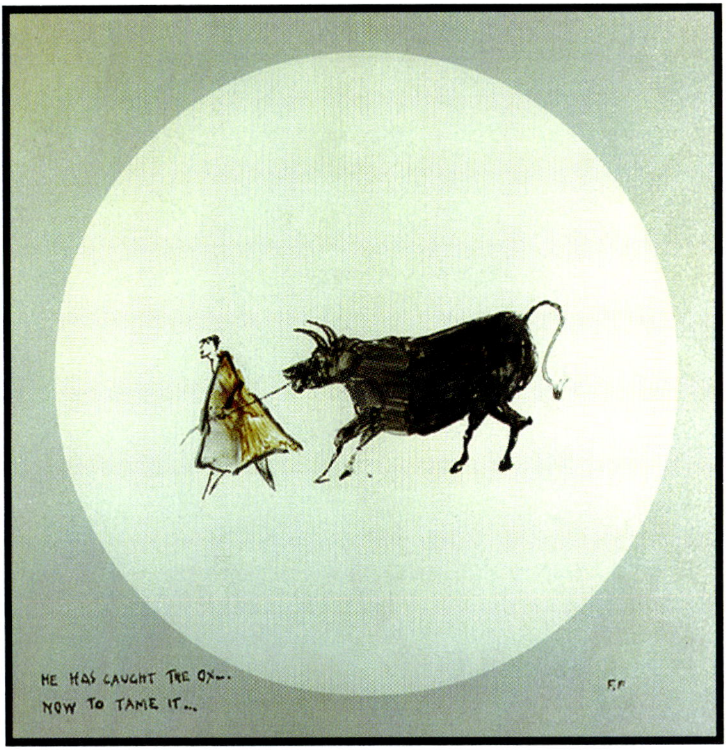
HE HAS CAUGHT THE OX...
NOW TO TAME IT...
F.F

HE HAS TAMED THE OX, RIDES HOME ON IT,
PLAYING HIS FLUTE...

F.F

THE OX HAS DISAPPEARED....

BOTH OX AND OXHERD
HAVE DISAPPEARED: GREAT

ALL THINGS HAVE BECOME NEW.

HE DESCENDS INTO THE MARKET PLACE BESTOWING BLESSINGS

The Way of the Cross and the Oxherding Pictures - as arranged with Mr. Dean Nims - will be on view at Pacem in Terris, 96 Covered Bridge Road, Warwick, N.Y. during the summer season. They are available for exhibition elsewhere from October to May. The first one of these exhibitions is scheduled for March 1996 at the Priory of the New Community Corporation, Newark and from mid-April to June 1, 1996 in the Cathedral of St. John the Divine, New York City.